The Royal Yacht
BRITANNIA

Foreword

The Royal Yacht *Britannia* was a proud and successful ambassador for Great Britain and the Commonwealth for over forty years. She dutifully served the Royal Family across the globe and played a key role in major historical events, including the handover of Hong Kong. It is little wonder that she still enjoys the enduring affection of the Royal Family, her former Officers and Yachtsmen, and those who saw her sailing into ports around the world.

It is a great honour for Edinburgh's historic port of Leith to be her permanent home. As well as proving popular with visitors, *Britannia* is being well maintained and has experienced considerable success as a leading visitor attraction. On behalf of my fellow Trustees, I would like to record our appreciation of the great work and unstinting efforts of our dedicated staff - we are all proud to be serving *Britannia*.

by the Chairman of
The Royal Yacht *Britannia* Trust,
Rear Admiral Neil Rankin CB CBE.

OFFICIAL GUIDEBOOK

Britannia in dry dock at Portsmouth, 1954

BUCKINGHAM PALACE

Together with members of my family, Prince Philip and I join you today to pay tribute to BRITANNIA and give our thanks to all who have been part of her Company. Looking back over forty-four years we can all reflect with pride and gratitude upon this great ship which has served the country, the Royal Navy and my family with such distinction. BRITANNIA has provided magnificent support to us throughout this time, playing such an important role in the history of the second half of this century. Steaming over one million miles she has proudly carried out over seven hundred Royal visits at home and overseas as well as numerous highly successful commercial programmes. Her achievements are a great testament to those who designed and built her and to those craftsmen and artisans who have maintained her with such dedication over all these years.

In recognising BRITANNIA's marvellous service, we pay particular tribute to the Officers and Royal Yachtsmen who have served in her. My family and I extend our heartfelt thanks to all these men for their unfailing loyalty, dedication and commitment to the Royal Yacht Service. While many of the present Royal Yacht's Company will return to the Royal Navy to continue their naval service and others come to the end of their service, we wish you every success in your future endeavours. We would also wish to thank the wives and families who have quietly but strongly supported the Royal Yacht over the years and often during the periods of long absence.

It is with sadness that we must now say goodbye to BRITANNIA. It is appropriate that with this final event she bows out in the style which is so typical of the manner in which her business has always been conducted.

Elizabeth R   _Philip_

11th December 1997.

Taken from the Paying-Off Ceremony, 11 December 1997

BRITANNIA, the last Royal Yacht

On 11 December 1997, at precisely one minute past three in the afternoon, The Queen was piped ashore for the final time from Britain's last Royal Yacht.

44 years earlier, The Queen had stood on a raised platform high above the Clydebank shipyard of John Brown & Co and pressed the button that launched Ship Number 691 into the Clyde.

Between those two occasions stretched an illustrious history of service that took *Britannia* the equivalent of once around the world for every year she sailed and made her the most famous ship afloat.

Britannia played host to the world's elite and was a powerful draw to the crowds who admired her wherever she went. In public, she was a living, working symbol of Royal Britain, whilst in private, away from the public eye, *Britannia* was the perfect sanctuary for The Queen and her family.

Now, as an award-winning visitor attraction and exclusive corporate events venue in Edinburgh, *Britannia* still retains a special magic. She provides a revealing insight into the lives of the Royal Family, their special guests and the dedicated ship's company.

Britannia at the Tower Bridge Centenary celebrations, 1994

The Queen's father, King George VI

Clyde-built

On 4 February 1952, an Admiralty telegram instructed the Clydebank shipyard, John Brown & Co, to 'proceed forthwith with detailed design and construction on fair and reasonable price basis of hull machinery of vessel referred to in your letter McN/MK dated 24th November'. This order was confirmed in writing the next day. Sadly, King George VI, The Queen's father, for whom the ship was being built, died just one day later on 6 February 1952. It then became The Queen's responsibility to oversee the commissioning of the new Royal Yacht.

John Brown & Co was one of the most famous shipyards in the world with an impeccable pedigree, having been responsible for the giant luxury liners *Queen Elizabeth* and *Queen Mary*. The building of *Britannia* began with the laying of the keel in June 1952.

Britannia was one of the last fully-riveted ships to be built. Her smooth-to-the-touch hull was achieved by the application of a special foundation layer and six coats of paint, and was a testament to the skills of John Brown's painters.

Just under a year after the hard work began, on 16 April 1953, the Royal Yacht was ready to be launched. The Yacht's name was a closely guarded secret right up until the last moment. On the day of the launch, The Queen revealed it to the waiting public with the words: 'I name this ship *Britannia*...'

Many coats of paint are applied to the hull

The Queen with Prince Philip at *Britannia's* launch

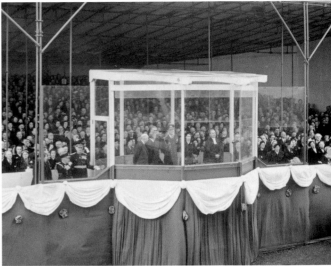

The Queen presides over the launching ceremony

 When The Queen released a bottle of Empire wine against *Britannia's* bow, it was the first time that a reigning monarch had launched a Royal Yacht built for their own use.

The crowds cheer *Britannia* down the slipway

Britannia *is special for a number of reasons. Almost every previous sovereign has been responsible for building a church, a castle, a palace or just a house. The only comparable structure in the present reign is* Britannia. *As such she is a splendid example of contemporary British design and technology.*

HRH Prince Philip

The Queen and Prince Philip arrive to launch *Britannia*

A very personal touch

Britannia was not only the Royal Yacht, she was very much The Queen's Yacht, such was her personal involvement in the design. Unlike Sandringham, Balmoral or any of the other residences which The Queen inherited, *Britannia* provided an opportunity for Her Majesty to make her mark on the finished form. The Queen and Prince Philip had a final say in many aspects of the design, creating a Royal residence that truly reflected their tastes, interests and style.

Sir Hugh Casson, the co-ordinating architect for the Festival of Britain, was chosen as the designer for the Royal Apartments. His lightness of touch resulted in a simple elegance, which has stood the test of time.

Sir Hugh Casson, the chosen designer for the Royal Apartments

Casson's original sketch of the State Dining Room

The Queen is a meticulous observer with very definite views on everything from the door-handles to the shape of the lampshades.

Sir Hugh Casson

Casson's original interior sketch for the State Drawing Room Anteroom

As a Naval Officer, Prince Philip took an active role in the technical aspects of the new Yacht. He also advised on which practices and traditions would be appropriate on a vessel fit for the 20th century.

Together, the Royal couple decided that the hull should be painted blue like their racing yacht *Bluebottle*, which had been given to them as a wedding present in 1948. This most visible aspect of *Britannia* set the new Yacht apart from her predecessors.

From broad aspects to small details, inside and out, *Britannia* became a living, floating reflection of the Royal personalities who would call her a home from home for the next 44 years.

Casson's original interior sketch for the State Drawing Room

The first of several Royal Navy ships to be named *Britannia*, at the Battle of Barfleur, 1692 (*Britannia* is right of centre)

A long tradition

Britannia was the last of 83 Royal Yachts reaching back to 1660 and King Charles II's *Mary*, a gift from the people of Amsterdam.

Britannia's predecessor, *Victoria & Albert III*, was built for Queen Victoria and was the first Royal Yacht not to be powered by sail. However, the monarch never stepped aboard after hearing rumours about the Yacht's lack of stability. Queen Victoria's successor, King Edward VII, had no such qualms, although his voyages were largely confined to local waters and the Mediterranean. *Victoria & Albert III* was to serve four sovereigns before ending her service in 1939.

For longer voyages, the Admiralty would either charter a liner or convert a major warship for Royal use. Clearly, if a new Royal Yacht was to be built to meet the demands of an outward-looking Britain, with strong ties to the Commonwealth, she would need to have a truly global reach.

There was general agreement that it would be prudent for a new Royal Yacht to be capable of providing a secondary function during wartime. After some debate, it was agreed that a vessel capable of speedy conversion into a hospital ship should be built. However, this was a role *Britannia* never fulfilled, missing out on the Falklands Campaign because of logistical problems with the type of fuel she used.

King Charles II's *Mary*

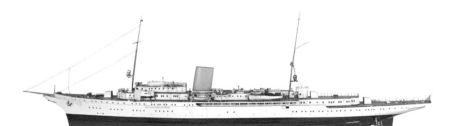

The German yacht *Grille*, rejected by King George VI as a suitable replacement for the ageing *Victoria & Albert III*

Victoria & Albert III

The decision had been taken to scrap V&A (Victoria & Albert) so I travelled to Portsmouth to salvage various items including the two binnacles. All the silver, linen and glass was also transferred to Britannia.

HRH Prince Philip

 Seven ships in the Royal Navy had carried the name *Britannia*, the first a 1703-ton warship dating back to 1682. Coincidentally, she finished her days as a hospital ship, the same role intended for the 'new' *Britannia* in time of war.

The binnacle from *Victoria & Albert III*

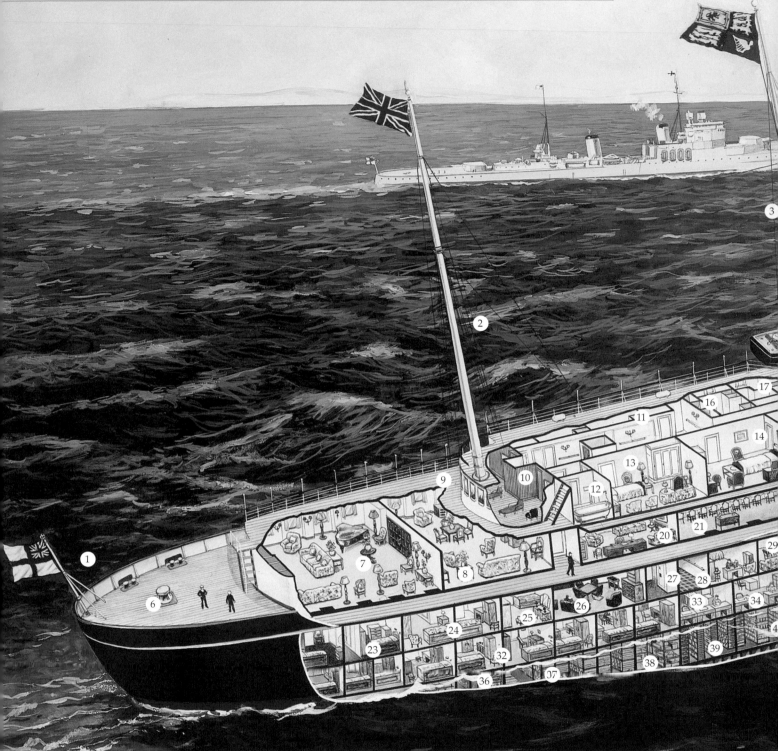

1.	Ensign Staff	13.	The Queen's Bedroom	25.	Master of the Household's Cabin
2.	Mizzen-Mast	14.	The Duke's Bedroom	26.	The Equerry's Sitting Room
3.	Mainmast	15.	The Duke's Bathroom	27.	Cloak Room
4.	Foremast	16.	Maid's Room	28.	Lower Entrance
5.	Jackstaff	17.	Maid's Room	29.	Guest Suite
6.	Quarter Deck	18.	Wardrobe Room	30.	Cabin
7.	The Drawing Room	19.	Valet's Bedroom	31.	Maid's Sitting Room
8.	The Anteroom	20.	The Queen's Sitting Room	32.	Staff Cabins
9.	Verandah Deck	21.	The State Dining Room	33.	Royal Clerks' Office
10.	The Sun Lounge	22.	Servery	34.	Clerks' Office
11.	Royal Bedrooms	23.	Staff Cabins	35.	Main Turbine Engine Room
12.	The Queen's Bathroom	24.	Royal Household Cabins	36.	Baggage Rooms

37. Linen Stores	49. Radar Scanner	61. Laundry
38. Blanket Stores	50. Royal Bridge	62. Yachtsmen's Mess
39. Wine Stores	51. Shelter Deck	63. Stabiliser Compartment
40. China Stores	52. Upper Deck	64. Engineers' Workshop
41. Fuel Tanks	53. Anchor Cables & Capstans	65. Chief Petty Officers' Cabin
42. Dinghies	54. Air Conditioning Plant	66. Upper Mess
43. Motor Boat	55. Ship's Doctor's Room	67. Stokers' Mess
44. Royal Barge	56. Sick Bay & Operating Theatre	68. Cold Rooms
45. Activity Boat	57. Boiler Rooms	69. Platform Deck
46. Jolly Boat	58. Bathrooms	70. Store
47. Compass Platform	59. Showers	71. Main Deck Mess
48. Officers' Cabins	60. Generator Room	72. Lower Deck Store Rooms
		73. Shipwrights' Workshop

An informal dinner during The Queen's Silver Wedding Anniversary cruise in 1972

This is where I can truly relax.

HM The Queen

The grand staircase leading to the Shelter Deck where the Royal Bedroom suites are found

Two ships in one

Britannia is really two ships in one. Forward of the mainmast is the operational side of the ship, where the Royal Navy Officers and Yachtsmen worked, and aft of the mainmast is where the Royal Apartments are situated.

The State Apartments in The Queen's other Royal residences, such as Buckingham Palace and Windsor Castle, are reserved for formal occasions. On *Britannia* the State rooms within the Royal Apartments were used every day and it is here that The Queen's own preference for the understated is revealed.

With their collection of personal possessions, including family photographs and furnishings from previous Royal Yachts, the Royal Apartments truly reflect Her Majesty's desire that '*Britannia* is to be at times the home of my husband and myself and of our family'.

15

The State Drawing Room has an air of informal elegance

The Waterford crystal glasses presented by John Brown & Co.

The State Drawing Room and Anteroom

Next to the State Drawing Room, the main reception room, is a smaller Anteroom where the Royal Family would assemble for drinks before lunch and dinner. Most of the furniture here was a gift from the Swedish Royal Family during a State visit to Stockholm in 1956. The antique mahogany bookcase and sideboard originate from the King's study in *Britannia's* predecessor, *Victoria & Albert III*. Taking pride of place in the bookcase, alongside the James Bond novels, is a set of Waterford crystal glasses and a tray presented by John Brown & Co., the shipyard that built *Britannia.*

The Anteroom is separated from the State Drawing Room by folding mahogany doors. The Drawing Room is large and comfortable, a place where the family could come together to relax with conversation, music and games. The Walmar baby grand piano is fastened to the floor by bolts in case of heavy weather. Probably the most notable name to 'sing for his supper' was Sir Noel Coward, invited to dine aboard during a Caribbean cruise by Princess Margaret.

At various other times, Diana, Princess of Wales, Princess Margaret and Princess Alexandra all entertained at the baby grand piano. For more formal occasions, a pianist from the Royal Marines Band provided suitably discreet background music. Cole Porter and Gershwin were particular favourites of The Queen.

Family entertainment centred around several card tables for bridge, whist or poker, as well as board games and the occasional large puzzle for the younger generation. A television set was housed in a specially-made cabinet, designed to blend in with the rest of the furniture.

The chintz sofas and armchairs, with covers originally chosen by The Queen, stand on a silver-grey carpet which runs the entire length of the State Apartments. It is partly covered by two stunning Persian rugs similar to those presented to The Queen during her visit to the Gulf States in 1979.

A portrait of Nelson hangs in the Anteroom

The overall idea was to give the impression of a country house at sea. I think we succeeded. Even today the Yacht looks very striking. She has an attractively old-fashioned air about her.

Sir Hugh Casson

The Anteroom with the bookcase from *Victoria & Albert III*

The Walmar baby grand piano in the State Drawing Room originally cost £350

The original plan for an open fire in the Drawing Room was scrapped due to a Naval regulation that a sailor would need to be stationed beside it with a bucket of water.

The State Dining Room also served as a place of worship on Sundays

The State Dining Room

The State Dining Room is the grandest room on board *Britannia* and was the prestigious setting for hundreds of spectacular banquets. Many famous names accepted the invitation to dine with The Queen, including Churchill, Thatcher, Mandela, Reagan, Clinton and Yeltsin; the guest list is a long and illustrious one.

The original centrepiece of the room was the 32-seater mahogany table and its Hepplewhite chairs. The table was made in five sections to allow different configurations depending on the occasion. For full-scale State banquets, the seating could be increased by adding two tables which came from *Victoria & Albert III*. Also brought on board from the previous Royal Yacht were four 19th century sideboards carved in the style of Chippendale.

Menu from Bangkok visit, 1997

Wooden shark carving from Pitcairn Island

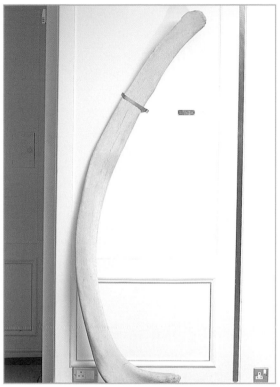
The whalebone collected by Prince Philip on Deception Island

The State Dining Room walls, display many items from around the world

For a State banquet the attention to detail would be meticulous. It could take up to three hours to set the dining table for 56 guests. The position of each item of cutlery and china was measured with a ruler to ensure perfection. Gracing the top table would be a pair of sculptured gold camels, said to be the single most valuable items on board. They were given to The Queen by the Ruler of Dubai on her visit to the Gulf in 1979.

The State Dining Room walls, painted white with a gold trim, display many interesting items including an array of exotic gifts and unusual mementoes of places visited. Some were given to The Queen, like a Sioux peace pipe from a visit to America, a sword dated 1738 given by the Swedish Navy and a Narwhal tusk, a gift from the Prime Minister of Canada. Other curiosities were collected, such as the two-metre long whalebone, which Prince Philip found on a beach on Deception Island.

Each alcove around the room has its own story to tell, such as the one containing a wooden carving of a shark from Pitcairn Island. It is signed on the back by all the adults living there in 1971, descendants of Fletcher Christian, the leader of the *Bounty* mutiny.

In another alcove there are ceremonial swords and daggers presented to the Duke of Edinburgh in the Gulf States in 1979. Above these is the long red strip of feather money presented to the Duke in 1957 in Santa Cruz.

The State Dining Room was not only for entertaining, it doubled as a cinema when on Royal duty and on Sundays was used for church services. On Princess Anne's 21st birthday the carpets were rolled up to reveal a hidden dance floor, which was put to good use for the first and probably last time on 2 August 1971.

The Queen's Sitting Room, where Her Majesty dealt with matters of State business

The Queen's Sitting Room

On the starboard side, between the State Dining and Drawing
Rooms, is The Queen's private Sitting Room. Here Her Majesty
worked at the green leather-topped desk for several hours
a day on State papers brought to her in distinctive red boxes.
These were flown or shipped out to *Britannia* wherever she
happened to be in the world. It was also the place where The
Queen held meetings with her Private and Press Secretaries,
as well as approving Royal Yacht matters like the day's menus.

The original sofa and armchair were used in two previous
Royal ships. The first was *HMS Vanguard* which took The
Queen (then a young Princess) and her parents to South Africa
for the first tour of that country by a reigning British monarch.
The second was *SS Gothic,* the Shaw Saville merchant ship,
which had been converted to be stand-in transport for the
Coronation Tour of 1953.

Above the fireplace the striking ornate gilt mirror, in the
style of a ship's wheel with carved figures of Neptune
and a mermaid, began its life in The Queen's Drawing Room
on the *SS Gothic*. The four wheatsheaf shaped wall lights,
one in each corner of the room, have the same origin.

The wall lights are designed in the shape of wheatsheaves

The gilt mirror is carved with figures of Neptune and a mermaid

20

The Duke's Sitting Room

The Royal telephones, identical to those in Buckingham Palace

Prince Philip's Sitting Room is on the port side. This 'study', as he preferred to call it, was also used by Prince Charles and, in contrast to The Queen's Sitting Room, has a masculine appearance with teak-panelled walls and a red leather-topped desk.

The Duke's Sitting Room was a convenient place for letter writing, quiet reading and meetings with his Private Secretary. Taking pride of place above the desk is a model of *HMS Magpie,* a reminder of the Duke's first naval command in 1951 when he was a Lieutenant Commander.

The Duke's and The Queen's quarters were connected by telephone to each other and to their respective Private Secretaries in offices on the deck below. The telephone system used on board was identical to that found at Buckingham Palace.

The model of *HMS Magpie* takes pride of place above the Duke's desk

The Duke's Sitting Room with model of *HMS Magpie*

The Queen's Bedroom with its original 1950s furniture

The Royal Bedrooms

On the Shelter Deck are four bedrooms, including those of The Queen and the Duke of Edinburgh. The windows here are higher to prevent any accidental glances from those passing along the deck outside. It is worth pointing out that never before has the bedroom of a living monarch been on view to the public in this way.

Built-in desk next to The Queen's bed

Both The Queen's and Prince Philip's Bedrooms are on the starboard side, with a connecting door between them. Each has its own bathroom, complete with thermometer to ensure that the Royal bathwater was at the right temperature. Whilst both bedrooms are undoubtedly modest in decor, each has its own particular character: The Queen's with its floral charm and the Duke's with darker timber furniture.

The Queen's Bedroom features an embroidered silk panel with a floral motif above the bed, specially commissioned in 1953. Her Majesty's bed-linen was from the *Victoria & Albert III*. The Duke's sheets were slightly smaller than The Queen's, who preferred a larger turnback, and on his explicit instructions were supplied with pillows that did not have lace borders.

 Joan Nicholson, a young British designer, was chosen by Sir Hugh Casson to design the silk embroidered panel. The Queen wanted the embroidery to remind her of home when she was travelling abroad, with hedgerows, wild flowers and butterflies. Ivory silk from France was chosen for the background and it took several workers many months to complete at the Royal School of Needlework in London.

Detail from Joan Nicholson's original watercolour design for the silk embroidery

Britannia's only double bed

A connecting door links Prince Philip's and The Queen's Bedrooms

Next to each bed is a panel with a buzzer to summon a steward should the need arise, day or night. During a State visit Her Majesty's Dresser could be very busy, with The Queen sometimes changing clothes up to five times a day. Her clothes, jewellery and accessories were kept in the wardrobe rooms on the same deck as the bedrooms. With the Prince being a Naval man, his particular concern was to ensure that the right medals or decorations were worn on every occasion.

There are two more bedrooms on the port side of the Shelter Deck, used by other members of the Royal Family. Probably the first people to use them were Prince Charles and Princess Anne as children. One of the rooms contains the only double bed on board and was the accommodation for the four Royal honeymoon couples who spent the first days of their married life on board *Britannia*.

Two decks below the Shelter Deck are a further sixteen cabins, each with its own en-suite facilities. Other members of the Royal Family, their guests and the Royal Household used these. The most senior guests, such as President and Mrs Clinton in 1994, were usually given the only suite of rooms on this level, namely Cabins 9 and 11, which are joined by a sitting room. The same suite was used by the last British Governor of Hong Kong, Mr Chris Patten, and his wife, on their return from the handover of Hong Kong in 1997. Before a voyage, The Queen always approved the accommodation arrangements and would take particular care to ensure that special guests had suitable reading material for their bedside table and plenty of fresh flowers to decorate the room.

Prince Philip's Bedroom with a darker timber finish

The Vestibule flooded by warm morning light

The Vestibule and Verandah Deck

A short walk aft from the Royal Bedrooms through the Vestibule
is the Sun Lounge and the wide expanse of the Verandah Deck, the
scene of many happy family occasions: the Royal children splashing
in a collapsible swimming pool, Prince Philip painting at his easel,
and games of quoits or deck hockey. It was also a ceremonial space,
used for State receptions and entertaining guests in fine weather.

Whatever the occasion, a constant presence was the imposing figure
of the ornate, intricately carved compass binnacle. This was one of
two rescued by Prince Philip from *Victoria & Albert III*, having
previously been relocated from Queen Victoria's *Royal George*.
It was a popular focal point for photographs taken by 'Snaps',
the crew member who acted as photographer.

The Verandah Deck was reinforced to take the weight of a helicopter
should *Britannia* have ever needed to fulfil her secondary role as
a hospital ship. As it turned out, this was never put to the test.

Prince Charles and his sons by the compass binnacle

The Sun Lounge is beautifully lined in teak panelling

The Sun Lounge

Between the Vestibule and the Verandah Deck
is The Queen's favourite room, the Sun Lounge,
where she and her family would take afternoon tea.

With its comfortable sofas and bamboo and wicker
chairs, it is a relaxed and informal room. Large
picture windows provide spectacular views over the
Verandah Deck and beyond. Cleverly concealed
cupboards contain a refrigerated drinks cabinet
and a record and games store. The line drawings
of former Royal Yachts on these cupboard doors
and the 'Rum Tot' tub dating from Queen Victoria's
era are reminders of *Britannia's* glorious lineage.

The rum tub was used until 1970 to issue the Yachtsmen's daily rum ration

The Rolls-Royce in its transporter

The Garage

When *Britannia* was built in 1953, a garage to house
The Queen's Rolls-Royce Phantom V or the Royal
Land Rover, was considered an absolute essential.
It was, however, not a straightforward task to get
a vehicle on board. The car, in its transporter, had
to be hoisted onto a special track that was fitted into
the deck. Even then, the Rolls-Royce could only be
squeezed into the Garage by removing its bumpers.
In more recent times a suitable car could usually
be found in the country that The Queen was visiting,
so the Rolls-Royce was rarely carried and the Garage
was put to use as a beer store.

Hoisting the Rolls-Royce on board was a complicated procedure

The Royal Barge was used to take The Queen and Prince Philip ashore

The Royal Barge

When *Britannia* was anchored in harbours around the world The Queen and Prince Philip would use the Royal Barge to travel to shore. The air-conditioned cabin was specially designed to ensure that the Royal party could be clearly seen as they approached the shore.

The Barge was built by Camper Nicholson in 1964 to replace the previous Royal Barge, which had originally belonged to the Royal Yacht *Victoria and Albert III*. It is 12.5 metres long and has two 125 horsepower engines which are capable of a maximum speed of 20 knots and when The Queen was on board, the Royal Barge would be crewed by five men.

Close up of a dolphin-fish on the Royal Barge

With a total of 10 boats and 18 life rafts, *Britannia* carried more craft than a warship. The 'activity boat' was often used to take the Royal Family ashore for private picnics and a fast motor boat was used to escort the Royal Barge whenever The Queen was on board.

Three generations of the Royal Family, 1989

The Queen and Prince Philip watch the Crossing-the-Line ceremony, 1970

The Royal Family gathers on the Verandah Deck during the last Western Isles cruise in 1997

The Queen cuts a ribbon to celebrate the One Millionth Mile ceremony, 1994

Younger members of the Royal Family on the Western Isles Tour, 1997

HMY . BRITANNIA
1,000,000 MILES
FEBRUARY. 1994.

Diana, Princess of Wales rushes to greet her sons, Toronto, 1991

Mrs Thatcher comes aboard in Melbourne, 1981

Presenting President and Mrs Reagan with a signed photograph, 1983

World Heads of State and Government pose for a photograph to commemorate D-Day, 1994

Britannia's nerve centre, the Bridge

The Bridge

The Bridge was the centre of command and control on board *Britannia*. But unlike any other ship, the orders given and decisions taken here affected the safety and well-being of one of the most important people in the world, The Queen.

Ultimately, overall responsibility rested with one man, *Britannia's* Captain. In recognition of this responsibility, *Britannia* was the only ship in the Royal Navy always commanded by an Admiral. The one exception to the rule was the last Captain, Commodore Anthony Morrow.

When *Britannia* was at sea, there would be an Officer of the Watch in overall charge, backed up by a Lookout and Signalman. Communication with the Helmsman on the deck below was via a metal voice pipe. To the rear of the Bridge is the Charthouse, where the Yacht's voyages were meticulously planned and plotted.

On the deck below is the Royal Bridge. Often, as *Britannia* sailed in or out of harbour, The Queen and the Duke of Edinburgh would wave to the cheering crowds on the quayside from here. The curved teak windbreak was a later feature, added for modesty's sake, to prevent sea breezes from lifting Royal skirts.

Metal voice pipe on the Bridge

The Wheelhouse

Britannia was steered and her engines controlled from the Wheelhouse, with commands given via two voice pipes from the Bridge. Normally, there would be three people manning the Wheelhouse, one at the ship's wheel and two to operate the brass telegraphs on either side of it. The telegraphs were linked via mechanical rod gearing to the Engine Room five decks below, passing on orders to regulate the ship's speed and movement.

Britannia's wheel has an interesting history. It had originally steered the racing yacht, also called *Britannia,* built for the Prince of Wales (later King Edward VII) in 1893. That Yacht had reached the end of her life and was scuttled south of the Isle of Wight by two Naval destroyers in 1936, but the wheel was saved.

Britannia's wheel, originally from King Edward VII's racing yacht of the same name

Britannia's boats suspended from their overhead davits

The Flag Deck

Behind the Bridge on the Flag Deck, the Signalmen sent messages to other ships, either by hoisting signal flags with the halyards (ropes) or with Morse code flashed from the signal lights.

As a global traveller, not only did the Royal Yacht carry an average of 2,000 different flags, but a certain amount of raw bunting was kept handy should a little creative flag-making be required due to changes in or damage to national flags. The most important flags were flown on the three main masts required by a Ship of State. When The Queen was on board, the flag of the Lord High Admiral (The Queen) was flown at the foremast, the mainmast flew the Royal Standard and the mizzen-mast displayed the Union flag.

Beneath the base of each of these hollow masts are two coins, a Coronation crown and shilling. These were placed when the masts were stepped (installed) in 1953. This was part of an age-old Naval custom, when payment was made to the angels to protect the souls of the sailors.

As *Britannia* would have to travel under bridges, the top 20 feet of the mainmast and the radio aerial had to be hinged. This was a feature unique to *Britannia* at the time. The nautical term for this hinging manoeuvre is 'scandalising'.

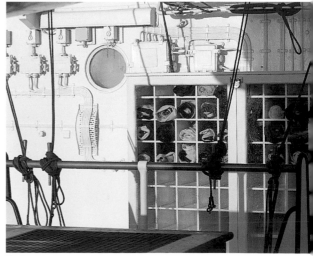

The flag locker storing the signal flags

The Admiral's day cabin is spacious and comfortable

The Admiral's Suite

Not only did the Admiral have ultimate responsibility for ensuring that *Britannia* ran like clockwork, but he was also in charge of a staff of some 20 Officers and 220 Yachtsmen. As befitted his standing, the Admiral's Suite contained the most spacious and comfortable rooms outside the Royal Apartments.

The Admiral's Suite is made up of a day cabin (with a sofa and armchairs from *Victoria and Albert III*), a sleeping cabin and a bathroom. The day cabin was for working, entertaining and sometimes eating meals. It was usual practice when The Queen, the Duke of Edinburgh or other members of the Royal Family were on board for the Admiral to dine with them in the State Dining Room.

The Admiral's sleeping cabin

When the Royal Family were not on board, the Admiral tended to eat alone in his room so that the other Officers could unwind without feeling they had to be on their best behaviour in front of their boss. However, the Admiral did his fair share of entertaining too, hosting dinners or drinks parties for special guests.

The sycamore-veneered wardrobes in the Admiral's sleeping cabin held his uniforms; he sometimes had to change up to 12 times a day, depending on his duties.

The Officers' Cabins were modest but comfortable

The Officers' Cabins

The Senior Officers' Cabins share a landing and corridor with the Admiral's Suite and the area was known as the 'Whispering Gallery', reflecting the need for quiet around their Commanding Officer. The Junior Officers' less spacious cabins were situated on the deck below.

The beds converted into sofas for use during the day and as well as being sleeping quarters, the small cabins doubled as offices. Here Officers would write reports and store files, uniforms and personal possessions. There was none of the luxury of an en-suite bathroom, however, with facilities being shared.

The First Lieutenant's Cabin

Dinners in the Wardroom were formal occasions

The Wardroom

Step into the Officers' Wardroom and you are entering the equivalent of a gentlemen's club. Here, *Britannia's* 20 Officers would assemble to dine and relax in an atmosphere steeped in tradition.

Dinner in the Wardroom was a splendid affair with the Officers dressed in their 'Red Sea Rig' comprising a white shirt, black trousers, patent leather shoes and cummerbund. Pre-dinner drinks would be served in the Anteroom adjacent to the Wardroom. On more formal occasions Officers would take it in turns to say Grace, delivered in rhyme, often with a healthy dose of irreverence. The meal was always accompanied by fine wines from *Britannia's* extensive cellar. At the end of the meal the loyal toast to The Queen was made and, if present, the Royal Marines Band might play the National Anthem. As a final touch, the 'Youngest Unheard Officer' was sometimes invited to deliver an amusing speech.

In the glass cabinets around the Wardroom and in the adjacent Anteroom is a collection of 19th and 20th century objects, some from previous Royal Yachts, and many gifts from *Britannia's* Officers.

One example is a silver Pegasus Bowl with flying horse handles depicting four previous Royal Yachts, presented to the Wardroom by the Officers of *Victoria & Albert III*. From the same source came a small but immeasurably valuable object: a gold button taken from the uniform of Admiral Lord Nelson. Another relic comes from further afield – a large, very elaborate silver salt cellar in the form of a sailing ship, reputedly owned by Russia's last Czar.

Precious metal: a small gold button from Nelson's coat hangs in the Wardroom Anteroom

The Anteroom where Officers could relax and unwind

The Wardroom Anteroom

With the bar as its focus, the Anteroom was where the Officers could relax after the tension and discipline of being 'front of house' in the eyes of the Royal Family and a watching world. Drinks, listening to the radio, Yacht quizzes and some very boisterous games assisted the unwinding process.

'Wombat Tennis' was perhaps the most infamous of these games. The 'ball', a soft-toy wombat, was donated by one of The Queen's Ladies-in-Waiting. The match began when the wombat was 'served' up into the ceiling fan and then batted from one side of the room to the other. Needless to say, the poor wombat was a regular visitor to the Sick Bay where the Ship's Doctor would stitch it back together to face the next game. Another creature to be found in various places around the room was a small wooden monkey. It arrived on board when The Queen visited Copenhagen in 1957. No Officer was officially allowed to touch it, but somehow the monkey was found in a different hiding place every day.

The 'Gin Pennant' was an important feature of the Anteroom. This was a small flag on a miniature flagstaff raised by an Officer to signal that the drinks were on him. Besides the light-hearted fun and banter, the Anteroom did take on a more dignified atmosphere when the Officers entertained The Queen and the Duke of Edinburgh, or other members of the Royal Family, for dinner or a drinks party.

Silver salt cellar from the last
Russian Czar

The Pegasus bowl depicts four former Royal Yachts

35

Warrant Officers' and Chief Petty Officers' Mess

In the Navy different ranks have their own recreation areas, known as Messes. As the most senior non-commissioned Yachtsmen on board, the Warrant Officers and Chief Petty Officers had their own Mess with separate sleeping quarters. When *Britannia* took The Queen on her annual holiday around the Western Isles of Scotland, protocol was rather more relaxed, and occasionally The Queen and other members of the Royal Family would join the Chief Petty Officers here for a drink.

Set into the walls of the Mess are two alcoves that originally contained figures of two British seafaring legends: Sir Francis Drake and Admiral Lord Horatio Nelson. Like all of the other Messes, the walls here are lined with signed photographs of the Royal Family.

Warrant Officers' and Chief Petty Officers' Mess

Petty Officers' and Royal Marines Sergeants' Mess

The Petty Officers and Royal Marines Sergeants had their own Mess with adjoining sleeping quarters. It was an extremely welcoming venue, so much so that an invitation to drink here was highly sought after by members of the Royal Household staff when they were on board.

Relaxing in the Mess

The Royal Marines Band performs Beat Retreat

The Royal Marines' Barracks

The 26 musicians of the Royal Marines Band Service were
Britannia's great entertainers. Their excellent musicianship
and impeccable drill captured the imagination of audiences
around the world.

Even President Reagan was moved to remark after viewing
their 30-minute Beat Retreat ceremony on a Californian quayside:
'Your Majesty, I thought Hollywood was the entertainment capital
of the world, but there's no way we could beat this'.

The Royal Marines also carried out other important duties.
In their starched whites, they were most visible as sentries
at the bottom of the gangway. They also held less public roles
such as regularly diving beneath *Britannia's* hull, when in
harbour, to check for anything suspicious.

The Marines' quarters (called 'Barracks') were extremely cramped
with very little storage space, a real problem for the bandsmen
who had to find space to store their uniforms and instruments,
as well as personal belongings.

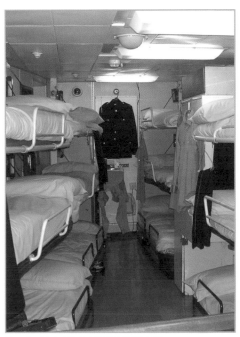

The cramped conditions of the Marines' Barracks

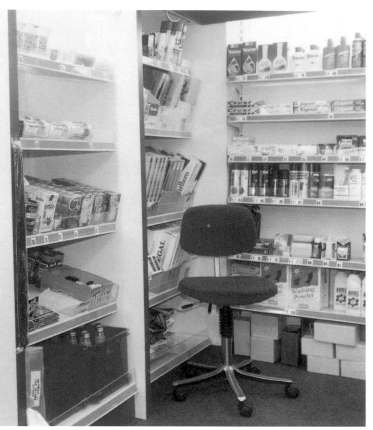

The NAAFI was the floating version of a corner store

The NAAFI

The NAAFI (Navy, Army and Air Force Institute) was the on-board shop. Open to everyone, it stocked basics such as confectionery, toothpaste, tobacco and a range of souvenirs unique to the Royal Yacht. These ranged from cut-glass whisky decanters and matching glasses to more modest T-shirts, pens and plaques, all bearing the *Britannia* crest and name.

The Royal children often visited to stock up on sweets. Diana, Princess of Wales, once bought a pale blue *Britannia* T-shirt for Prince William.

This on-board shop still trades and is part of the tour. It sells homemade fudge, sweets and drinks, which are much enjoyed by visitors.

The Mail Office

Britannia was away from home for long stretches, often voyaging to the other side of the world, and her Mail Office provided a vital service for keeping in touch with family and friends. These were the days before mobile phones, so wherever *Britannia* berthed, the arrival of the mailbags was eagerly awaited.

When The Queen was on board, her official mail would be flown or shipped out from London to *Britannia* every day. Then, the ship's mail would join the 'Royal Mail' and the Officers and Yachtsmen could send and receive post daily via the Buckingham Palace Court Postmaster.

The Mail Office, a vital link with family and friends

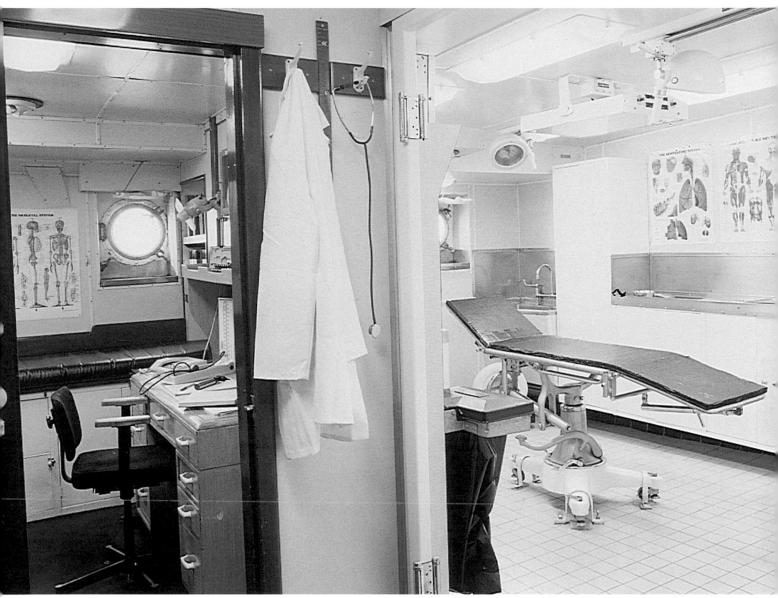

The Doctor's Consulting Room, looking into the Operating Theatre

The Sick Bay and Operating Theatre

When the plans for the Royal Yacht were approved by The Queen early in 1952, they incorporated the idea that *Britannia* should be able to be converted to a hospital ship during times of conflict. It was estimated that up to 200 patients could be accommodated in wards in the aft part of the ship where the Royal Apartments were located.

A dental surgery, anaesthetic rooms and X-ray equipment, as well as other specialist facilities such as a physiotherapy room and a pathology laboratory, were also planned. The objective was to convert from Royal Yacht to hospital ship in a mere 24 hours.

In 1992, it was finally decided that the casualty and medical care needs of a modern Navy could be better met elsewhere and therefore this secondary role for the Royal Yacht ceased.

The Yacht's regular medical facilities incorporated a Sick Bay with accommodation for two patients in cot-beds and another two bunks contained within a bench seat. There was also a Doctor's Consulting Room and an Operating Theatre. The Ship's Doctor would look after the health of the Officers and crew, whilst The Queen always had a Royal Physician on board to care for her.

Britannia's Laundry was far larger than that of other Navy ships of a similar size

The Laundry

There were two reasons why the Royal Yacht was the only ship in the Royal Navy to have such a large Laundry and one that was permanently manned by her own crew. Firstly, if ever converted into a hospital ship, there would be a need for greater capacity than normal. Secondly, with *Britannia's* 240 Officers and Yachtsmen changing uniform up to six times a day when on Royal duty, there was clearly a need to deal with an enormous amount of laundry. The washing machines, dryers and steam presses used to work around the clock. Up to 600 shirts could be processed in a single day.

The Laundry also took care of the Royal washing, although a strict rota kept this separate from the Yachtsmen's clothes. On one occasion the Royal washing turned an unexpected shade of blue (and Her Majesty's Dresser turned an angry shade of purple). The cause was quickly traced to a chemical reaction in the pipes, remedied by adjusting the pH value of the water.

This was a very uncomfortable place to work, with temperatures rising as high as 45° Celsius, (120° Fahrenheit). It certainly made an impression on Prince Charles: 'I always admired those characters who worked in such heat'.

The Galleys

On *Britannia* there are three Galleys: one for the Officers, one for the Yachtsmen and one for The Queen and Royal Household.

When the Royal Family was on board their food was always prepared by chefs from Buckingham Palace who were especially flown out to the ship. Before *Britannia* set sail, the ship's holds and storerooms were stocked with fresh, frozen and dried provisions. The coldrooms could hold two months' supply of fish and meat, and the dairy and vegetable rooms held enough provisions to feed the whole ship for a month. Fresh bread was baked daily, and whenever possible local vegetables were bought to supplement supplies.

There was a special cold room that was referred to as the 'Jelly Room', for it was in here that the Royal children's jellies were stored.

For formal occasions the three-course menus were usually printed in French long before the voyage began, but every morning The Queen would approve the day-to-day menus that were printed on board.

The Galleys were capable of turning out large quantities of meals: a hundred chickens could be roasted simultaneously in the huge Admiralty ovens, whilst the enormous four-tiered steamer had no problem producing 200 puddings in a single batch.

Stirring the Christmas pudding in *Britannia's* galley, 1991

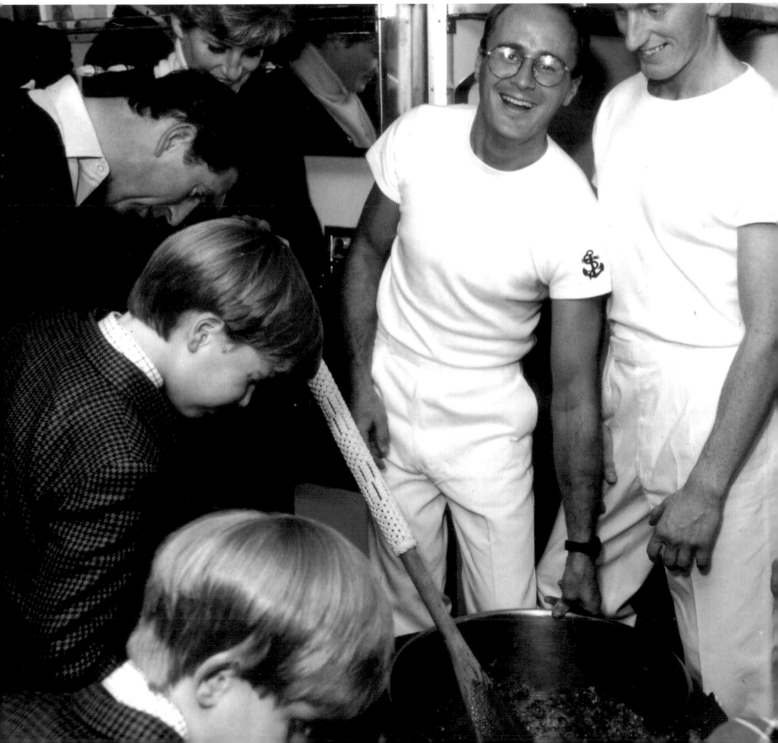

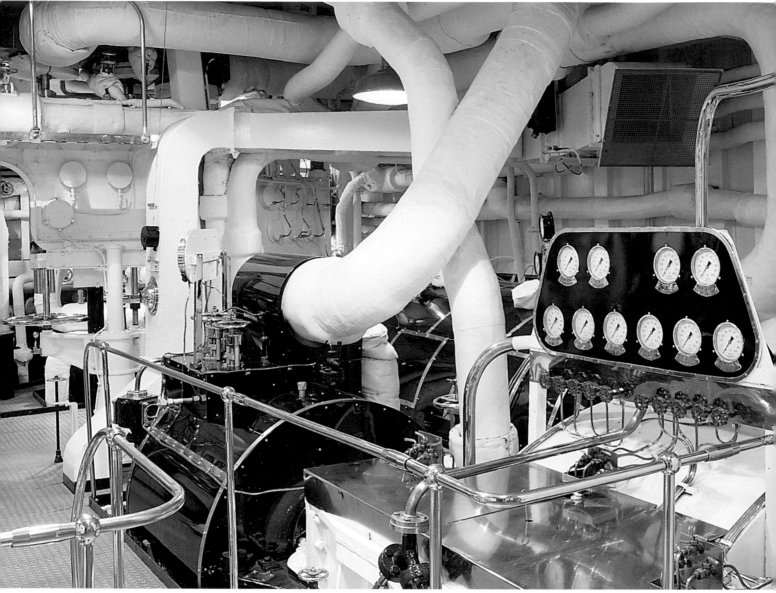

Two pairs of steam turbines powered *Britannia*

The Engine Room

This Engine Room is quite unlike any other. It had a mat outside, not to wipe one's feet when leaving, but to do so when entering. This immaculate world of white enamel, polished chrome, brass and gleaming black steam turbines has barely changed since 1953. Little wonder that during his visit to *Britannia* in 1992, America's General Schwarzkopf was heard to remark, 'Okay, I've seen the museum piece. Now, where's the real engine room?'

The engines have steamed 1,087,623 nautical miles, with barely a problem. They turned out a total of 12,000 horsepower and drove *Britannia*, with her four-bladed propellers, to a maximum of 22.5 knots.

Visitors to the Engine Room invariably asked to see the 'golden rivet', said to be secretly driven into every great ship in the dead of night. To satisfy their curiosity, one was improvised with the application of gold leaf on an existing rivet. On decommissioning, it was found that the rivet had been moved to the other side of the Engine Room.

Britannia's Engine Room has barely changed since 1953

The Generator and Boiler Rooms

The Boiler Room next to the Engine Room was where the power for the Royal Yacht was generated. A pair of Foster Wheeler 'D' Type boilers initially burned furnace fuel before being converted to diesel in 1983. From here, the steam passed through large white pipes to drive the Engine Room's turbines. Their power went to the gearboxes, which drove the ship's propellers via 30 metre-long shafts.

Electricity for the Yacht came from a trio of turbo-steam generators. Back-up emergency power could be provided by a diesel generator (nicknamed 'Chitty Chitty Bang Bang'), rumoured to have been the oldest in active service in the entire Royal Navy. This engine originally drove *HM Submarine Vampire*.

This was not the only piece of equipment with a history: some of the water distillers were from the battleship *HMS Queen Elizabeth* which took part in the Dardenelles Campaign of 1915.

The Boiler Room supplied the steam which drove *Britannia's* turbines

Britannia's electricity needs could be satisfied by any two of the three turbo generators

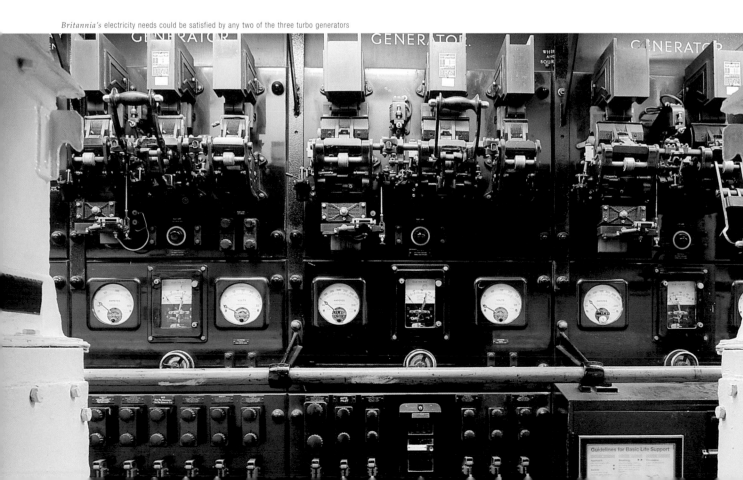

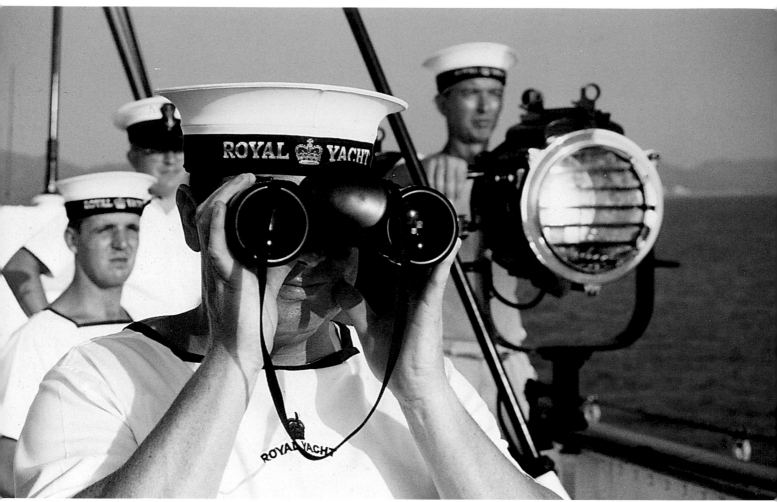

Signalling duty on the Flag Deck

Plotting a course

A crew apart

Britannia's 20 Officers and 220 'Yotties' were part
of the Royal Navy, but in many ways they were apart
from it – in ethos, custom and practice. After all, this
was no ordinary vessel: constantly in the public eye,
charged with the security of the Royal Family and
dedicated to achieving 'unobtrusive excellence'
in everything she did. This took absolute attention
to detail with little or no room for error, which
included taking three hours to set the table with
inch-perfect precision for a State banquet, or
ensuring that the slope of the Royal gangway
never exceeded 12 degrees.

Everything was done to preserve the Royal
tranquillity. Consequently, most orders were not
given verbally, but by hand signal; soft soled
plimsolls were worn and any work near the
Royal Apartments had to be completed by 08:00.

 If any urgent changes were made to the daily orders
that regulated every minute of life on board, they would
be posted on the 'red-hot' notice boards throughout the
Yacht. Woe betide any crewman who did not pay
close attention.

The Queen with some 'Yotties', South Pacific Tour, 1977

Around half of the ship's company were appointed for a two-year tour of duty. The rest of the crew were hand picked for permanent service and remained with *Britannia* throughout their Naval career, accepting this post for the honour and privilege of serving The Queen.

Service on the Royal Yacht attracted no extra pay, allowances or leave. There was not much chance of promotion either, as this was only possible if someone left the Royal Yacht Service, which was extremely rare. Yachtsmen could also face instant dismissal for misconduct.

Even when they were ashore, the Royal Yachtsmen were set apart, having to wear collar and tie after 18:30. In contrast to this formality, all ratings were called by their first names (or nicknames). And there was the opportunity to join in the traditional end-of-cruise variety concerts in front of the Royal Family.

My abiding memory is not of places, but of people, the Royal Yachtsmen, a ship's company who have no equal. I felt I could call on them to do anything and it would be done, cheerfully, efficiently and quietly.

Lord Lewin

A rare moment of mass relaxation during The Queen's 1961 cruise to Africa

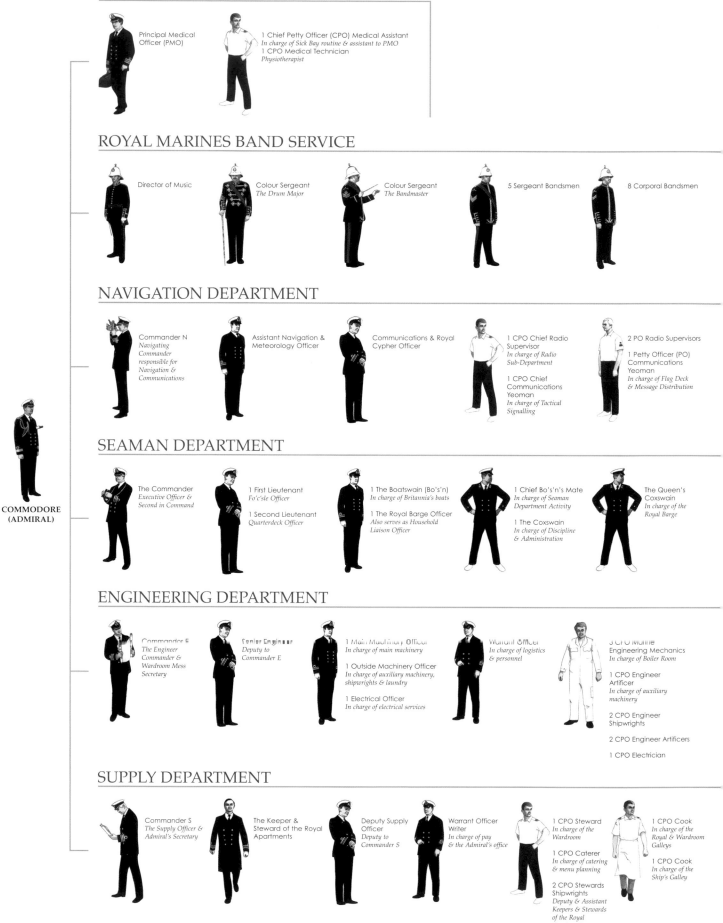

MEDICAL DEPARTMENT

Principal Medical Officer (PMO)

1 Chief Petty Officer (CPO) Medical Assistant
In charge of Sick Bay routine & assistant to PMO
1 CPO Medical Technician
Physiotherapist

ROYAL MARINES BAND SERVICE

Director of Music

Colour Sergeant
The Drum Major

Colour Sergeant
The Bandmaster

5 Sergeant Bandsmen

8 Corporal Bandsmen

NAVIGATION DEPARTMENT

Commander N
Navigating Commander responsible for Navigation & Communications

Assistant Navigation & Meteorology Officer

Communications & Royal Cypher Officer

1 CPO Chief Radio Supervisor
In charge of Radio Sub-Department
1 CPO Chief Communications Yeoman
In charge of Tactical Signalling

2 PO Radio Supervisors
1 Petty Officer (PO) Communications Yeoman
In charge of Flag Deck & Message Distribution

SEAMAN DEPARTMENT

The Commander
Executive Officer & Second in Command

1 First Lieutenant
Fo'c'sle Officer

1 Second Lieutenant
Quarterdeck Officer

1 The Boatswain (Bo's'n)
In charge of Britannia's boats

1 The Royal Barge Officer
Also serves as Household Liaison Officer

1 Chief Bo's'n's Mate
In charge of Seaman Department Activity

1 The Coxswain
In charge of Discipline & Administration

The Queen's Coxswain
In charge of the Royal Barge

ENGINEERING DEPARTMENT

Commander E
The Engineer Commander & Wardroom Mess Secretary

Senior Engineer
Deputy to Commander E

1 Main Machinery Officer
In charge of main machinery

1 Outside Machinery Officer
In charge of auxiliary machinery, shipwrights & laundry

1 Electrical Officer
In charge of electrical services

Warrant Officer
In charge of logistics & personnel

3 CPO Marine Engineering Mechanics
In charge of Boiler Room

1 CPO Engineer Artificer
In charge of auxiliary machinery

2 CPO Engineer Shipwrights

2 CPO Engineer Artificers

1 CPO Electrician

SUPPLY DEPARTMENT

Commander S
The Supply Officer & Admiral's Secretary

The Keeper & Steward of the Royal Apartments

Deputy Supply Officer
Deputy to Commander S

Warrant Officer Writer
In charge of pay & the Admiral's office

1 CPO Steward
In charge of the Wardroom

1 CPO Caterer
In charge of catering & menu planning

2 CPO Stewards Shipwrights
Deputy & Assistant Keepers & Stewards of the Royal Apartments

1 CPO Cook
In charge of the Royal & Wardroom Galleys

1 CPO Cook
In charge of the Ship's Galley

COMMODORE
(ADMIRAL)

Who's who in *Britannia*

As with all Royal Navy Ships, the Captain (Commodore or Admiral in *Britannia's* case) was in charge, supported by his staff of up to 20 Officers and 220 Yachtsmen. Although *Britannia's* complement could vary depending on the Yacht's duties.

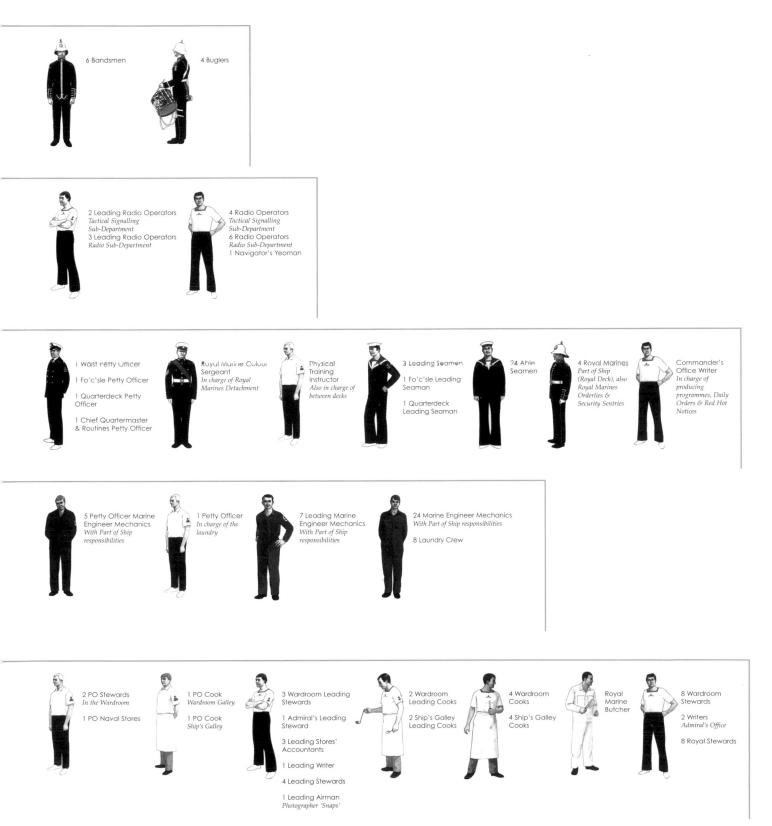

6 Bandsmen

4 Buglers

2 Leading Radio Operators
*Tactical Signalling
Sub-Department*
3 Leading Radio Operators
Radio Sub-Department

4 Radio Operators
*Tactical Signalling
Sub-Department*
6 Radio Operators
Radio Sub-Department
1 Navigator's Yeoman

1 Waist Petty Officer

1 Fo'c'sle Petty Officer

1 Quarterdeck Petty Officer

1 Chief Quartermaster & Routines Petty Officer

Royal Marine Colour Sergeant
In charge of Royal Marines Detachment

Physical Training Instructor
Also in charge of between decks

3 Leading Seamen

1 Fo'c'sle Leading Seaman

1 Quarterdeck Leading Seaman

24 Able Seamen

4 Royal Marines
Part of Ship (Royal Deck), also Royal Marines Orderlies & Security Sentries

Commander's Office Writer
In charge of producing programmes, Daily Orders & Red Hot Notices

5 Petty Officer Marine Engineer Mechanics
With Part of Ship responsibilities

1 Petty Officer
In charge of the laundry

7 Leading Marine Engineer Mechanics
With Part of Ship responsibilities

24 Marine Engineer Mechanics
With Part of Ship responsibilities

8 Laundry Crew

2 PO Stewards
In the Wardroom

1 PO Naval Stores

1 PO Cook
Wardroom Galley

1 PO Cook
Ship's Galley

3 Wardroom Leading Stewards

1 Admiral's Leading Steward

3 Leading Stores' Accountants

1 Leading Writer

4 Leading Stewards

1 Leading Airman
Photographer 'Snaps'

2 Wardroom Leading Cooks

2 Ship's Galley Leading Cooks

4 Wardroom Cooks

4 Ship's Galley Cooks

Royal Marine Butcher

8 Wardroom Stewards

2 Writers
Admiral's Office

8 Royal Stewards

A floating nursery

From practically her first voyage, *Britannia* became a playground for generations of Royal children. It was customary for each Royal child to be allocated a 'Sea Daddy' from the crew to look after them while on board. The ship's company ensured that there was never a shortage of amusements: treasure hunts, picnics ashore and water fights using syringes from the sick bay.

However, even the patience of the most dedicated Yachtsman was tried when a young Prince Charles kicked his football over the side off the Isle of Man, not just once, but twice. Needless to say, *Britannia* didn't turn back to collect it the second time.

It wasn't all play though. The Royal children had their 'chores' to do too: helping to clean life rafts, stirring the ship's enormous Christmas pudding and even taking a (highly supervised) hand at the wheel.

Princess Anne has a Royal Yacht 'sailing' lesson, 1954

 After the fun of the day, the Royal children had their meals separately from the adults – even at that early age they were learning the formality and etiquette that was to become second nature in later life.

The young Princes Andrew and Edward, Viscount Linley and Lady Sarah Armstrong-Jones practice their saluting

Peter Phillips lends a hand slipping anchor with his 'Sea Daddy', 1968

Prince Charles performing in a concert on board *Britannia*, 1970

*We found as children that
there was so much to do, we
expended so much energy that
we couldn't describe our time
in the Yacht as a rest.*

HRH Princess Anne

Appropriately enough on a Yacht so familiar with
ceremony, the young Princes Andrew and Edward
and their cousins, Viscount Linley and Lady Sarah
Armstrong-Jones, tried out as officers. However,
their Naval saluting left much to be desired, having
been copied from the guards at Buckingham Palace.

Britannia at the Cowes Week Regatta in 1996

Western Isles

The Royal summer plans followed a well-established pattern and *Britannia* played a key role. The Royal Yacht would first appear at the Cowes Week Regatta off the Isle of Wight, where Prince Philip and other members of the Royal Family would exercise their passion for yacht racing. Then *Britannia* would set sail for the Western Isles of Scotland for The Queen's annual holiday cruise. While the Royal Family was cruising, the Royal Household would move from Buckingham Palace to their northern home at Balmoral to prepare for the arrival of The Queen and her family.

Visiting the outlying parts of western Scotland on a leisurely cruise away from the crowds allowed The Queen and her family to relax and unwind. It meant barbeques ashore on deserted beaches, quiet walks and informal concert parties organised by the Yachtsmen.

Another traditional part of the cruise was to anchor off Scrabster, in order to visit The Queen Mother at the Castle of Mey. It was also a time when The Queen would invite the Officers to dine with her. The Officers would reciprocate with a dinner for The Queen and Prince Philip in the Wardroom.

The Queen, Prince Andrew and Prince Edward wave as they leave Portsmouth at the start of the Western Isles cruise in 1991

Sharing a joke off the Isle of Mull

She (The Queen) got a week or ten days of sanctuary from anything that was going on. That little bit of tranquillity made up for all the other things that she had to do... it was a chance to have her family around her in her environment.

The Duke of York

The Queen Mother greets The Queen at Scrabster harbour, 1996

Honeymoon hideaway

There could not have been a more ideal venue for a Royal honeymoon. Secluded from the public eye and able to cruise to out-of-the-way places, *Britannia* played host to four Royal honeymoons.

The first newlyweds, Princess Margaret and Anthony Armstrong-Jones, visited the Caribbean in 1960 for a month, anchoring off small islands and enjoying picnics ashore.

In 1973 Princess Anne and Captain Mark Phillips also chose the Caribbean for their honeymoon. With the world's press dogging their every move, the Yacht's company had their work cut out to ensure the privacy of the Royal couple. On more than one occasion, they resorted to the ruse of sending a decoy barge to a beach to throw the press photographers off the trail.

 Princess Anne's honeymoon cruise got off to a rocky start with twenty-foot waves sending the Royal couple to their bed with a bad case of seasickness.

The first honeymooners: Princess Margaret and Anthony Armstrong-Jones

Princess Anne takes a photograph while on honeymoon with Captain Mark Phillips, 1973

The Prince and Princess of Wales on their honeymoon

In 1981, the Prince and Princess of Wales boarded *Britannia* in Gibraltar to begin their 16-day honeymoon around the Mediterranean. It was a thoroughly informal time, at least as far as the young Princess was concerned. She enjoyed exploring the lower decks and, on one notable occasion, joined the Yachtsmen in an impromptu sing-song, including 'What shall we do with the drunken sailor?'

It was five years later that *Britannia's* final honeymoon cruise took her to the Azores. On board were the Duke and Duchess of York. Once again, the press were kept at bay and the time spent together aboard *Britannia* made for happy memories: 'After all the organisation of the things that we had to do, to be able to have four or five days of complete peace and quiet was fantastic', the Duke recalled.

The perfect romantic retreat

I was in the scullery washing up when I heard a voice in the servery. I went out to look, to find a newly-wed Princess sitting on the freezer in a bikini, flip flops and hat, licking a choc ice.

Leading Steward Mark Elliot

Britain afloat

Britannia was the first, and indeed the last, truly global Royal Yacht. Wherever in the world she went, a little bit of Britain went too. During almost 44 years of service, *Britannia* made over 700 overseas visits to just about every corner of the globe. From the Amazon River to the St Lawrence Seaway, from the South Sea Islands to New York City, *Britannia* was a powerful symbol of Britain and all it stood for.

For citizens of the Commonwealth, who saw *Britannia* a total of 223 times, the Royal Yacht was both a link with their colonial past and a reminder of their ongoing relationship with the United Kingdom. As The Queen herself remarked at the launch, speaking of her late father:

'For he felt most strongly, as I do, that a yacht was a necessity and not a luxury for the Head of our great British Commonwealth, between whose countries the sea is no barrier, but the natural and indestructible highway.'

For many citizens of far-flung Commonwealth countries, the distinctive blue-hulled presence of *Britannia*, gleaming and immaculate from bow to stern, was as close to a vision of Britain as they could ever hope to see.

 How do you arrive gleaming in port after a long sea voyage? Make sure you head for the nearest rainstorms on route, rinsing off the salt and leaving beautifully shining sides.

On the Royal Bridge, with President Eisenhower during the opening of the St Lawrence Seaway in 1959

Britannia in the sunshine off the Cayman Islands, 1984

On the jetty, there was a huge crowd and there were bands playing. Suddenly, around the Spithead came the sight of this amazing ship with the Royal Marines Band playing on the top deck, flags flying, and The Queen and the Duke of Edinburgh on deck waving to the crowds. It was so proud-making, beautiful and British.

Lady Susan Hussey
The Queen's Lady-in-Waiting

Meeting President Mandela in Cape Town, 1995

Prince Charles is met by His Highness, the Crown Prince in Doha, Qatar, 1997

Royal returns

As the pressure to justify the costs of maintaining a Royal Yacht grew more acute, it was felt that *Britannia* should play a more commercial role as a venue for British overseas trade missions. An invitation to come on board for what became known as 'Sea Days' proved irresistible to the world's leading business and political figures, especially on those occasions when a member of the Royal Family was present.

A British businessman bidding for part of a £4 billion Chinese steel contract vividly described one example of *Britannia's* unique attraction to Rear-Admiral Garnier, 'He told me that all the people he wanted to see were on his table, including the relevant Chinese Government Minister, the Mayor and the Project Manager ... it would have taken him another six months to a year to have done that without a Sea Day!'

From the very first Sea Day in Rio in 1968, to the final one, hosted in Gibraltar on 22 July 1997, *Britannia's* allure earned Britain and its companies a very healthy return. Commercial contracts are generally too confidential for a precise figure, but the Overseas Trade Board estimated that £3 billion had been made for the Exchequer as a result of commercial days between 1991 and 1995 alone. As the ultimate in 'networking' venues, *Britannia* had clearly proved her status as an invaluable asset on the UK's trade balance sheet.

Princess Alexandra presents an award during an investiture in Tokyo in 1997

Commodore Anthony Morrow escorts Margaret Beckett, Minister for Trade and Industry on her visit to *Britannia* in Japan, 1997

Britannia *was invaluable for this kind of event. We wanted to have the top business leaders in attendance and an invitation to dinner on the Royal Yacht was seldom refused, particularly when spouses were included.*

Lord Michael Forsyth

Britannia's boats pick up evacuees from Aden, South Yemen

Mercy mission

After 30 years of service, *Britannia* had yet to fulfil her secondary role as a hospital ship. However, as she sailed down the Red Sea in January 1986, en route to Australia, she was asked to play the equally challenging role of rescue ship.

Civil war had broken out in South Yemen, and ships were urgently required to evacuate British nationals and others trapped by the fighting. As a non-combatant Royal Navy ship, *Britannia* would be able to enter territorial waters without further inflaming the conflict. The Queen swiftly gave her full backing and the State Dining and Drawing Rooms were cleared to welcome a new type of guest.

At 20:00 on 17 January 1986, the Yacht, with a large Union Flag flying at each mast and her superstructure floodlit so no-one could mistake her identity, dropped anchor off Khormakasar Beach. The first of *Britannia's* boats headed for shore to begin the shuttle of evacuees back to the refuge of the Royal Yacht.

When *HMS Newcastle* discovered that a dog was amongst those rescued, their carpenters made a wooden lamp-post which was sent across to the Yacht.

After being given a blanket, hot soup and a snack, the refugees were shown to dormitories improvised within the State Apartments.

Over the next six days, the Yacht's boats rescued 1,068 of the 1,379 people of 55 nationalities saved by British ships during what became known as Operation Balsac.

Often operating under fire from the opposing sides, her crew thoroughly deserved the telegrams of praise that later streamed in from The Queen, the Prime Minister, the Foreign Secretary and all the defence chiefs.

The State Drawing Room and Anteroom welcome a new type of guest

When I saw the launch coming in, with its White Ensign fluttering in the wind, I was very happy inside and there were tears in my eyes. The Queen's Yacht turned back for me, just for me!

Yemen-born London bus driver, Saleh Ali

British evacuees from Aden arrive safely back in Britain

A long goodbye

Britannia's final and most widely televised role was at the handing over of Hong Kong, at the stroke of midnight on 30 June 1997. After the Union Jack was lowered for the last time, she slipped out of Hong Kong Harbour, carrying the last Governor, Chris Patten. With her final Royal duty completed, this symbol of the British Commonwealth could head back to home waters for the last time.

On 10 October 1997, the new Labour Government announced that there would be no replacement for, or refit of, *Britannia*. It was the same grave news that had been read out to the whole ship's company by Rear-Admiral Woodard in the State Dining Room three years previously.

In the years leading up to 1997, there had been rumours that a new Royal Yacht might be commissioned. Political opinion had been mixed. The argument for *Britannia's* trade role was made by some. The Ministry of Defence had actually been considering some fairly advanced plans, with an estimated construction bill of £80 million.

Chris Patten leaves Hong Kong with the Union Jack under his arm

Hong Kong marked *Britannia's* last official visit to a foreign port

Commodore Anthony Morrow watches as Prince Charles greets Tony Blair before the handover of Hong Kong

For the last time, *Britannia* sails into Portsmouth

On 20 October 1997, *Britannia* left Portsmouth on her final operation: a farewell tour of the UK. In a clockwise circumnavigation of Britain, *Britannia* visited six major ports, including Glasgow.

Having said her goodbyes, *Britannia* hoisted the traditional paying-off pennant. This usually measures one and a half times the length of the ship plus one foot for every year of service, but as this would have been too unwieldy it was decided to make it 412 feet, the Yacht's length.

With pennant flying in a dramatic thunderstorm, the last Royal Yacht sailed from London on 21 November 1997 for a final night at sea as she headed for her decommissioning port, Portsmouth. She docked the next morning and at 11:35, the Engine Room heard their last orders as the call came to stop engines. *Britannia's* Royal career was over.

The final shut down of the engines

Saying farewell to *Britannia* was emotional for everyone

Fond memories

Fourteen members of the Royal Family attended *Britannia's* official decommissioning ceremony in Portsmouth on 11 December 1997, to bid farewell to a vessel that had become so much part of their family.

Before the decommissioning service, the Royal Family went on board for a walk around the Yacht and said a personal good-bye to the ship's company. A final lunch was eaten in the Royal Apartments and then The Queen was piped ashore for the last time at 15:01.

Besides the dignitaries, gathered at the quayside for the service were 2,200 former Royal Yacht Officers and Yachtsmen, together with their families. Around the UK, millions watched on television. After the three principal Naval Chaplains had completed the formal service, it was left to the Band of Her Majesty's Royal Marines Portsmouth to pay the final tribute to *Britannia*.

Looking back over 44 years we can all reflect with pride and gratitude upon this great ship which has served the country, the Royal Navy and my family with such distinction. Britannia has provided magnificent support to us throughout this time, playing such an important role in the history of the second half of this century.

HM The Queen

The Queen leaves the Royal Yacht for the very last time in Portsmouth, 11 December 1997

As the band marched off, they struck up 'Auld Lang Syne' and saluted the Yacht.

Many a tear was shed, not just by The Queen and the Princess Royal, but also by more than one hard-bitten former Yachtsman. As The Queen's Private Secretary put it: 'It was a very moving occasion because everyone was saying good-bye to something they all loved, from The Queen downwards'.

In April 1998, the Government revealed the results of the hotly-contested competition between several UK cities to secure the Yacht. Six months later, the Royal Yacht welcomed her first new visitors on board in the port of Leith, Edinburgh. What was once The Queen's private retreat was now well and truly in the public domain.

Britannia approaches Edinburgh's historic port of Leith for her final berth

The Royal Yacht *Britannia* Trust

When it was announced that *Britannia* was to be preserved, and not scuttled as most previous Royal Yachts, cities in the UK were invited to submit proposals to purchase *Britannia*. The purchase price was set at £250,000 and bids were judged on their quality, appropriateness and how each would ensure that *Britannia* was maintained in keeping with her former role.

The proposal to bring *Britannia* to Edinburgh was prepared by Forth Ports PLC as part of their plans to regenerate the historic port of Leith. Following the success of the Forth Ports bid, the company donated all of the necessary funds required to purchase *Britannia* and undertake the works required to make her accessible to the public.

On 29 April 1998, ownership of *Britannia* transferred from the Ministry of Defence to The Royal Yacht *Britannia* Trust, which is a registered charity.

The Trust's role is to maintain and preserve *Britannia* in keeping with her former role and to display her to the public as an example of British maritime history. All funds generated go towards this worthy cause and the Trust receives no public subsidy.

The Trust's first chairman was Viscount Younger of Leckie KT KCVO TD DL (former Secretary of State for Defence). He was succeeded by Rear Admiral Neil Rankin CB CBE, who took over the post in January 2003.

On arrival in Edinburgh on 5 May 1998, *Britannia* went into dry dock for a comprehensive refurbishment. This involved making the four upper decks accessible for wheelchairs, repainting, and changing over to shore-based services such as electricity, water and drainage. A temporary Visitor Centre was constructed in Leith's Western Harbour and this was to be *Britannia*'s home until she moved to her permanent berth in September 2001.

The ever popular *Britannia*, now a successful visitor attraction, Ocean Terminal, Leith

Visitors to *Britannia* can tour five decks

Britannia no longer has 220 Royal Yachtsmen devoted to her upkeep and wellbeing. Now a dedicated team of 12 expert staff, led by a Naval Architect, ensure that she is maintained to the highest standards. Most of this in-house team have either a Royal Navy or Naval Dockyard background.

Marine surveyors carry out an independent survey of all areas above and below decks every year and the Yacht's hull is inspected annually by qualified divers. It is expected that *Britannia* will need to go into dry dock every ten years or so, when the hull below the water line will be scraped and repainted.

Britannia is now a member of the Core Collection of the National Register of Historic Vessels, the official register of the most important British ships still in existence.

The uniform of the Royal Marines Bandsmen now on display in the Visitor Centre

Britannia opened to the public on 19 October 1998 and received extensive media coverage around the world. Almost everything visitors to *Britannia* see today is original and on loan from The Royal Collection, the Ministry of Defence and the *Britannia* Wardroom Officers Trust.

In the first year *Britannia* attracted over 400,000 visitors, twice as many as originally expected. Now *Britannia* attracts approximately 300,000 visitors annually, making her one of the most popular visitor attractions in Scotland.

When *Britannia* moved to her final berth next to Ocean Terminal in 2001, much of the Main Deck was opened to the public, showing more of the working side of the ship in contrast to the State Apartments. The audio handset tour now covers five decks, with highlights including the Royal Bedrooms, the State Dining Room and the Engine Room.

Maintenance team

In addition to being a popular visitor attraction, *Britannia* is also a successful corporate hospitality venue. The exclusive dinners and receptions reflect *Britannia's* former international trade mission role. On average, *Britannia* hosts 80 such events a year.

Britannia has a Scottish Tourist Board Five Star rating and has received numerous awards, including Condé Nast Johnsens' Most Excellent Venue 2004 and runner-up Best UK Visitor Attraction Gift Shop 2004.

Britannia is maintained to the highest standards

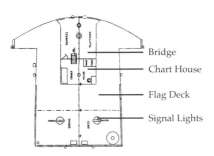

Bridge
Chart House
Flag Deck
Signal Lights

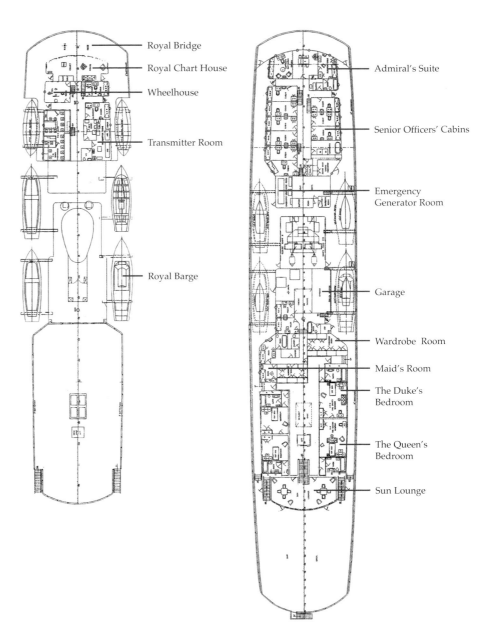

Royal Bridge
Royal Chart House
Wheelhouse
Transmitter Room
Royal Barge

Admiral's Suite
Senior Officers' Cabins
Emergency Generator Room
Garage
Wardrobe Room
Maid's Room
The Duke's Bedroom
The Queen's Bedroom
Sun Lounge

Compass Platform   Bridge Deck   Shelter Deck

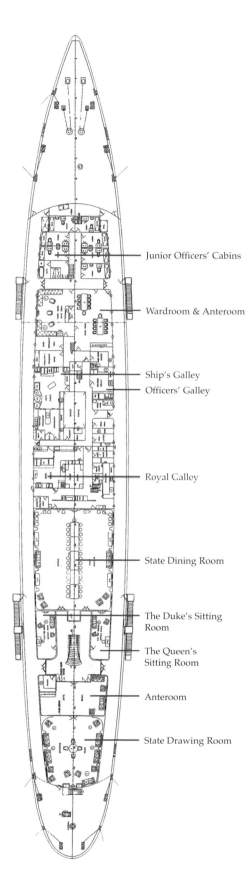

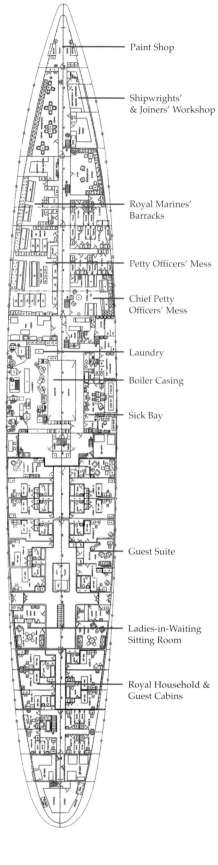

Paint Shop

Shipwrights' & Joiners' Workshop

Royal Marines' Barracks

Petty Officers' Mess

Chief Petty Officers' Mess

Laundry

Boiler Casing

Sick Bay

Guest Suite

Ladies-in-Waiting Sitting Room

Royal Household & Guest Cabins

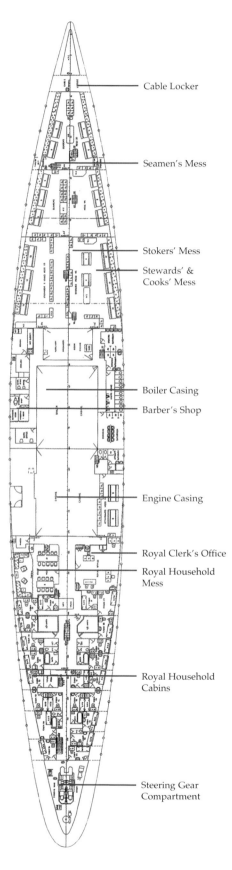

Cable Locker

Seamen's Mess

Stokers' Mess

Stewards' & Cooks' Mess

Boiler Casing

Barber's Shop

Engine Casing

Royal Clerk's Office

Royal Household Mess

Royal Household Cabins

Steering Gear Compartment

Junior Officers' Cabins

Wardroom & Anteroom

Ship's Galley
Officers' Galley

Royal Galley

State Dining Room

The Duke's Sitting Room

The Queen's Sitting Room

Anteroom

State Drawing Room

Upper Deck

Main Deck

Lower Deck

BRITANNIA DOSSIER

Laid down:
John Brown & Co. Ltd, Clydebank

Designer/Builder:
Sir Victor Shepheard, Director of Naval Construction;
and John Brown & Co. Ltd

Launched:
16th April 1953 by HM Queen Elizabeth II

Commissioned:
At sea, 11th January 1954

Length overall:
125.65m or 412ft 3in

Length on waterline:
115.82m or 380ft

Length between perpendiculars:
109.73m or 360ft

Maximum breadth moulded:
16.76m or 55ft

Breadths at upper deck moulded:
16.61m or 54ft 6in

Depth moulded to upper deck 45ft abaft midships:
9.90m or 32ft 6in

Depth moulded to upper deck at fore perpendicular:
12.29m or 40ft 4in

Depth moulded to upper deck at after perpendicular:
10.31m or 33ft 10in

Load displacement:
4,715 tons

Mean draft at load displacement:
5.2m or 15ft 7in

Gross tonnage:
5,862 tons

Shaft horsepower:
12,000

Speed:
22.5 knots maximum, 21 knots continuous

Engines:
Two geared steam turbines, developing a total of 12,000
shaft horsepower. Two main boilers and an auxiliary boiler
for harbour requirements, by Foster Wheeler

Range:
2,196 miles at 20 knots (burning diesel fuel)
2,553 miles at 18 knots (burning diesel fuel)

Mainmast Height:
42.44m or 139ft 3in - Royal Standard

Foremast Height:
40.54m or 133ft - Lord Admiral's Flag

Mizzen-Mast:
36.22m or 118ft 10in – Union Flag

Fuel & Water:
330 tons of fuel oil providing a range of 2,000 miles
at 20 knots 120 tons of fresh water. Additional tanks
can increase fuel capacity to 490 tons and fresh
water capacity to 195 tons

Propeller Diameter:
3.12m or 10ft 3in

Pitch:
2.74m or 9ft

Developed blade area:
$5.17m^2$ or $55.7ft^2$

Tip clearance from hull:
0.84m or 2ft 9in

Maximum rudder torque:
125 tons ft at 14 knots astern and 30.5° angle

Rudder torque at 22 knots:
69 tons ft at 35° angle

Rudder torque at 15 knots:
33 tons ft at 35° angle

Maximum normal rudder force:
63.5 tons at 22 knots ahead, and 25.5 tons at 14 knots astern

Acknowledgements

Illustrations by Jim Proudfoot: *p.46 & 47*

Illustration by John Marshall: *p.12 & 13*

© Sir Hugh Casson Ltd. By kind permission of Carola Zogolovitch from original watercolour drawings by Hugh Casson RA:
p.9 (top, middle & bottom)

On board photographs by Eric Thorburn: *p.15, p.16 (top), p.17 (top, middle & bottom), p.19 (middle & bottom), p.20 (top, middle & bottom),
p.21 (top, middle & bottom), p.22 (top & middle), p.23 (top, middle & bottom), p.24 (top), p.25 (top & bottom), p.27 (bottom),
p.30 (top, middle & bottom), p.31 (top & bottom), p.32 (top & bottom), p.33 (top & bottom), p.34 (top & bottom),
p.35 (top, bottom left & bottom right), p.42 (top & bottom), p.43 (top), p.65 (top)*

© UK Crown Copyright / MOD. Reproduced with the permission of the Controller of Her Majesty's Stationery Office:
*p.26 (top), p.27 (top), p.28 (top right & middle), p.29 (middle left & right), p.37 (top), p.41, p.45 (top), p.49 (bottom), p.51 (top), p.52 (bottom),
p.53 (bottom), P56, p.57 (top & bottom), p.69 (bottom)*

PA / EMPICS: *Front cover, p.2, p.7 (bottom), p.28 (bottom left & right), p.29 (bottom), p.36 (bottom), p.50 (top & bottom), p.51 (bottom),
p.52 (top), p.53 (top), p.55 (top), p.58 (bottom), p.59 (bottom), p.60 (bottom), p.61 (top & bottom), p.62, p.63 (top & bottom), back cover*

With the permission of The Trustees of the Imperial War Museum, London: *p.24 (bottom), p.26 (bottom), p.44 (top & bottom),
p.45 (bottom), p.48 (top), p.49 (top), p.54, p.55 (bottom), p.58 (top), p.59 (top), p.60 (top & middle), p.69 (top)*

National Maritime Museum, London: *p.10 (top & bottom left)*

RIBA Library Photographs Collection: *p.8 (bottom)*

Photograph by Patrick Lichfield / Camera Press London: *p.14*

Photograph by Diana Memorial Fund / Camera Press London: *p.29 (top)*

Photograph by Yousuf Karsh / Camera Press London: *p.8 (bottom)*

Jayne Fincher: *p.28 (top left)*

Lucy Quinton: *p.19 (top left), p.37 (bottom right), p.65 (right middle & right bottom)*

Photography © Andy Gray Digital: *p.64*